The Christmas Story

Copyright © 2023 by The Salvation Army USA Southern Territory

All rights reserved. This book or any portion thereof may not be reproduced or used in any manner whatsoever without express written permission of the publisher except for the use of brief quotations in a book review.

For information write:
The Salvation Army
USA Southern Territory
Literary Council
1424 Northeast Expressway
Atlanta, GA 30329

Scripture taken from the Holy Bible, New International Version®, NIV®. Copyright© 1973, 1978, 1984, 2011 by Biblica, Inc.™ Used by permission of Zondervan. All rights reserved worldwide. www.zondervan.com The "NIV" and "New International Version" are trademarks registered in the United States Patent and Trademark Offices by Biblica, Inc.™

Welcome to a unique way of exploring the Christmas story. I have been inspired to write this because I enjoy journaling and coloring as I reflect on the Scriptures. For me it helps to enhance the experience. Art therapy has been a proven method for retention of information as well as relaxation. This book is designed to be journaled. There are blank pages for notes, doodles or grand works of art, coloring pages that were inspired by each chapter, and a few prompts to help you to immerse yourself in the story. I hope you enjoy this experience.

How to Journal in this book
The journal prompts are designed to enhance the reading and give you the opportunity to put your thoughts into words or pictures as you reflect on the Scripture. This is an opportunity to relax and let your creativity flow!

Suggested materials
Colored pencils will work best and if you are new to this medium. I recommend looking up some blending exercises to try on the page provided.

Crayons are a great option for any kind of art journaling. They are vibrant, inexpensive, and easy to use.

Markers are also a good choice for bold colors; however, you may experience some bleed through from the back side of the page. This may not bother you, if so, great, but if it does, feel free to prepare your page ahead of time with some gesso. Just make sure to put some scrap paper underneath the page you're working on or else you will paint your book shut (don't ask how I know this).

I hope you enjoy this book and make the most of it as you spend some time *Drawing from the Word* this Christmas!

Introduction

Christmas is a special time- that might just be the most obvious statement ever. We often drive ourselves crazy trying to make it the most special ever. There are thousands of ideas floating around on how to make this happen. It can be stressful or overwhelming. Oddly enough, all the stress and insanity that comes with this holiday is self-imposed. There is no right or wrong way to "do Christmas."

My brother and sister and I grew up in a house where Christmas was the climax of the year. We had the tree, hosted the parties, went to the parades, acted in the church plays, decorated the yard, and baked the cookies. I can feel the tension start to mount just typing that list!

When we became adults and had children of our own, my sister gave up on Christmas. It was a huge shock to our family. My mother felt betrayed. Her holiday rebellion became a regular topic of discussion in our family gripe sessions. In a way I understood why she would make such a bold decision. After all, who needs a new baby and all the holiday chaos? She just needed a break. A few years into her Christmas protest she explained just that. So, I asked her what her favorite Christmas memories were from when we were kids. She shared with me that her favorite thing was when we'd get in the van as a family and drive around and look at Christmas lights together, drink hot chocolate and sing Christmas songs as a family. She enjoyed it because it was simple, and it was just us. No preparations or need for perfection.

I shared my favorite Christmas memory with her. It was one year when we didn't have anything. There were no gifts, no parties. We were very young. Our mother tried hard to make it special. She made us dinner with "fancy jello" for dessert (fruit and whipped cream-yum!). Then she took a length of tinsel, taped it to the wall of the trailer in the shape of a triangle and we spent the evening cutting pictures out of magazines to tape to the paneling inside the tree. Our mother turned down the lights and, as the snow fell silently outside, she read us the Christmas story from the enormous family Bible that was only for special occasions.

This Christmas stands out the most because we didn't spend it rushing around trying to find the perfect gifts or stressing about the decorations. We spent it together. It is because of that Christmas that the biblical account of the first Christmas has become sacred to me. It was the only gift we got that year and the only thing we really needed. This book is a celebration of those quiet meaningful moments we find amid the holiday to focus on what's truly important.

This book is dedicated to Cindie, and Josh.
May your Christmases remain sacred and
may your dangly-downs always sparkle.

The Christmas Story from Luke 1

The Birth of Jesus Foretold

[26] In the sixth month of Elizabeth's pregnancy, God sent the angel Gabriel to Nazareth, a town in Galilee, [27] to a virgin pledged to be married to a man named Joseph, a descendant of David. The virgin's name was Mary. [28] The angel went to her and said, "Greetings, you who are highly favored! The Lord is with you."

[29] Mary was greatly troubled at his words and wondered what kind of greeting this might be. [30] But the angel said to her, "Do not be afraid, Mary; you have found favor with God. [31] You will conceive and give birth to a Son, and you are to call Him Jesus. [32] He will be great and will be called the Son of the Most High. The Lord God will give Him the throne of His father David, [33] and He will reign over Jacob's descendants forever; His kingdom will never end."

[34] "How will this be," Mary asked the angel, "since I am a virgin?"

[35] The angel answered, "The Holy Spirit will come on you, and the power of the Most High will overshadow you. So, the Holy One to be born will be called the Son of God. [36] Even Elizabeth your relative is going to have a child in her old age, and she who was said to be unable to conceive is in her sixth month. [37] For no word from God will ever fail."

[38] "I am the Lord's servant," Mary answered. "May your word to me be fulfilled." Then the angel left her.

The Christmas Story from Luke Chapter 1

Mary Visits Elizabeth

[39] At that time Mary got ready and hurried to a town in the hill country of Judea, [40] where she entered Zechariah's home and greeted Elizabeth. [41] When Elizabeth heard Mary's greeting, the baby leaped in her womb, and Elizabeth was filled with the Holy Spirit. [42] In a loud voice she exclaimed: "Blessed are you among women, and blessed is the Child you will bear! [43] But why am I so favored, that the mother of my Lord should come to me? [44] As soon as the sound of your greeting reached my ears, the baby in my womb leaped for joy. [45] Blessed is she who has believed that the Lord would fulfill His promises to her!"

The Birth of Jesus Foretold

Mary's Song

⁴⁶ And Mary said:

"My soul glorifies the Lord
⁴⁷ and my spirit rejoices in God my Savior,
⁴⁸ for He has been mindful
of the humble state of His servant.
From now on all generations will call me blessed,
⁴⁹ for the Mighty One has done great things for me—
holy is His name.
⁵⁰ His mercy extends to those who fear Him,
from generation to generation.
⁵¹ He has performed mighty deeds with His arm;
He has scattered those who are proud in their inmost thoughts.
⁵² He has brought down rulers from their thrones
but has lifted up the humble.
⁵³ He has filled the hungry with good things
but has sent the rich away empty.
⁵⁴ He has helped His servant Israel,
remembering to be merciful
⁵⁵ to Abraham and his descendants forever,
just as He promised our ancestors."
⁵⁶ Mary stayed with Elizabeth for about three months and then returned home.

The Christmas Story from Luke Chapter 1

Much has been written about Mary and the supernatural experience she had. Try to put yourself into her shoes. What was it like to be suddenly standing before an angel? Not only an angel, but one with such an incredible greeting? Who was she that one of the heavenly hosts addressed her as "highly favored?" In the Scriptures angels often say, "Do not be afraid," but I imagine that these encounters are terrifying. Not only is Mary confronted by a godly messenger, but she is also given news she never expected. She was pregnant even though she was a virgin! She had some questions. Anyone would have.

What impresses me most about Mary in this scripture passage is the answer she gives in verse 38.: "I am the Lord's servant," Mary answered. "May Your word to me be fulfilled."

What a tremendous faith to stand before the angel Gabriel, after hearing such jaw-dropping news. I may have been more like Moses and put up a little argument first, but not Mary. She understood that though she was in a difficult position by human standards, it was a great honor to be chosen by God and so she accepted her role in His plan.

Then Mary went to her cousin, Elizabeth's house. Elizabeth and her husband were godly people. Obviously with divine knowledge, Elizabeth's greeting to her young cousin must have been of great comfort to the young girl. After all, how was she supposed to explain all that had happened to her older and wiser relative about being pregnant out of wedlock? God took care of that for her. The Holy Spirit told Elizabeth and she seems to instantly understand that this was an incredible thing that happened to Mary.

The Birth of Jesus Foretold

God is like that. I have found that during the hardest, most frustrating times of obedience in my life, when trying just doesn't seem like it will be enough that even the worst time seems to work. I know that He is watching out for me. We might not be as pious and humble as Mary, but we can be assured that He is always there, helping us when we need it the most.

The Christmas Story from Luke Chapter 1

Take some time to pray and reread Mary's song. Let her words wash over you and tell the Lord what is on your heart in this moment.

What is the key verse for you in this passage?

_____
_____
_____
_____
_____
_____
_____
_____

Has there ever been a time in your life where you just didn't know how it was going to work out?

_____
_____
_____
_____
_____
_____
_____
_____

The Birth of Jesus Foretold

Looking back, can you see how God was with you and provided a way through?

_____

_____

_____

_____

_____

_____

_____

_____

_____

_____

_____

_____

_____

_____

_____

_____

_____

_____

The Christmas Story from Luke Chapter 1

Sometimes it is hard to see Him working when we are amid confusion, but even if the situation didn't turn out the way we wanted it to, we can be assured that God is in control. If we put our faith and hope in Him, He will see us through anything that comes our way.

Deuteronomy 31:6 says, "Be strong and courageous. Do not be afraid or terrified because of them, for the Lord your God goes with you; He will never leave you nor forsake you."

Journal your thoughts here.

_____

_____

_____

_____

_____

_____

_____

_____

_____

_____

_____

_____

The Birth of Jesus Foretold

Matthew 1:18-25

[18] This is how the birth of Jesus the Messiah came about: His mother Mary was pledged to be married to Joseph, but before they came together, she was found to be pregnant through the Holy Spirit. [19] Because Joseph her husband was faithful to the law, and yet did not want to expose her to public disgrace, he had in mind to divorce her quietly.

[20] But after he had considered this, an angel of the Lord appeared to him in a dream and said, "Joseph son of David, do not be afraid to take Mary home as your wife, because what is conceived in her is from the Holy Spirit. [21] She will give birth to a son, and you are to give him the name Jesus, because he will save His people from their sins."

[22] All this took place to fulfill what the Lord had said through the prophet: [23] "The virgin will conceive and give birth to a Son, and they will call Him Immanuel" (which means "God with us").

[24] When Joseph woke up, he did what the angel of the Lord had commanded him and took Mary home as his wife. [25] But he did not consummate their marriage until she gave birth to a son. And he gave Him the name Jesus.

The Christmas Story

Matthew 1:18-25

The book of Luke doesn't mention the angel appearing to Joseph. No one really knows why, but it is recorded in the book of Matthew. Again, we see how God is looking out for Mary and for the whole family. God sent an angel to speak to Joseph and explain things so that Joseph stays with her and raises Jesus as his own.

We see in these few short verses that Joseph was an honorable man. After finding out that wife was pregnant, he devised a plan to deal with her discreetly, so as not to cause either of them any embarrassment. He really had every right to blame and point fingers, but he chose to divorce her quietly. This speaks of his character and helps us to understand why he was chosen for this task in the first place. The Scripture says he decided on this course of action because he was faithful man. He would have been seeking to do things not in his own interests, but in the ways that God would have him to do them.

Before he can carry out his plans, however, the Lord sent an angel to clarify the situation. The angel explained how the Baby is part of God's great prophecy to save humankind from their sins. And so, Joseph, being a man of faith, did as the angel instructed. He stayed with Mary and named the child Jesus.

In this passage we see how God knows our thoughts and intentions before they ever become words or actions. He knew the plan that Joseph was devising, and while it was a kind way of handling the situation, God had a different plan for his life. In verse 23, the angel refers to the prophecy found in Isaiah 7:14, "Therefore the Lord Himself will give you a sign: The virgin will conceive and give birth to a son, and will call Him Immanuel."

The Christmas Story

As a godly and faithful man, Joseph would have been familiar with this prophecy and its significance. He would have understood in that moment that this wasn't any ordinary child and that, just like Mary, he was being blessed, rather than put in an inconvenient situation.

Sometimes when we forget to consult God, because we think we know what's best for us, we can charge ahead and miss a blessing. His plans don't always make the most sense because they are beyond our understanding, but when we trust Him, we can be assured that He will bless us for it. Romans 8:28 tells us "And we know that in all things God works for the good of those who love him, who have been called according to His purpose."

Look over your answers from the previous section and take some time to pray before considering these questions.

Like Joseph, what solid plan have you had in place and then had to take a leap of faith instead?

_____

_____

_____

_____

_____

_____

_____

_____

Matthew 1:18-25

Is there a situation you are facing that you need to let go of and give over to God?

The Christmas Story

It isn't always the easiest thing to do, to put all your faith and hope in God, but just like with Joseph, we can be assured that if we do, that He will make a way through and that He has a plan for your life.

Spend some time in prayer and if you decide to let go of whatever you are currently facing, write your prayer here so that you can come back to it and see what God is doing for you.

Journal your thoughts here.

_____

_____

_____

_____

_____

_____

_____

_____

_____

_____

_____

_____

_____

Matthew 1:18-25

From Luke 2

The Birth of Jesus

In those days Caesar Augustus issued a decree that a census should be taken of the entire Roman world. ²(This was the first census that took place while Quirinius was governor of Syria.) ³ And everyone went to their own town to register.

⁴ So Joseph also went up from the town of Nazareth in Galilee to Judea, to Bethlehem the town of David, because he belonged to the house and line of David. ⁵ He went there to register with Mary, who was pledged to be married to him and was expecting a child. ⁶ While they were there, the time came for the baby to be born, ⁷ and she gave birth to her firstborn, a Son. She wrapped Him in cloths and placed Him in a manger, because there was no guest room available for them.

⁸ And there were shepherds living out in the fields nearby, keeping watch over their flocks at night. ⁹ An angel of the Lord appeared to them, and the glory of the Lord shone around them, and they were terrified. ¹⁰ But the angel said to them, "Do not be afraid. I bring you good news that will cause great joy for all the people. ¹¹ Today in the town of David a Savior has been born to you; He is the Messiah, the Lord. ¹² This will be a sign to you: You will find a Baby wrapped in cloths and lying in a manger."

¹³ Suddenly a great company of the heavenly host appeared with the angel, praising God and saying,

¹⁴ "Glory to God in the highest heaven, and on earth peace to those on whom His favor rests."

The Christmas Story

¹⁵ When the angels had left them and gone into heaven, the shepherds said to one another, "Let's go to Bethlehem and see this thing that has happened, which the Lord has told us about."

¹⁶ So they hurried off and found Mary and Joseph, and the Baby, who was lying in the manger. ¹⁷ When they had seen Him, they spread the word concerning what had been told them about this child, ¹⁸ and all who heard it were amazed at what the shepherds said to them. ¹⁹ But Mary treasured up all these things and pondered them in her heart. ²⁰ The shepherds returned, glorifying and praising God for all the things they had heard and seen, which were just as they had been told.

²¹ On the eighth day, when it was time to circumcise the child, He was named Jesus, the name the angel had given Him before He was conceived.

In this part of the story, Jesus is born. It is only mentioned in verses six and seven, but Mary might tell us that there was much more to the story than that. In these verses we learn that she was to give birth in a city foreign to her and that they had no room to stay in. So, we find the Messiah being wrapped and laid in a manger. The first part promise had been fulfilled. Mary gave birth to the Son of God.

Soon after His birth, Jesus gets some unlikely guests. There were shepherds nearby tending to their sheep that night, when again the good news is brought by angels. Unlike the angels that appeared to Mary and Joseph who came to them individually and delivered a personal message, these were many angels. I imagine them filling the sky and lighting it up brighter than the noon sun. They were praising God together and sharing the excitement with these men. They decided to go down and find the Baby and see Him for themselves. How could they turn down an invitation like that?!

The Christmas Story

When we initially meet the shepherds, they are at work. There would have been a lot of shepherds working that evening as people were gathered to be counted for the census and would not have left their flocks at home. They represented "every man." The angels did not go to the palace or the Temple to announce the birth of Jesus, but instead went to these 'average Joes' and invited them to join in the festivities. That was a hallmark of Jesus' ministry on earth. He made it obvious that He wasn't interested in someone's status or wealth, but who they were as a person. He called fishermen and tax collectors to be in His personal circle. It wasn't by mistake that lowly shepherds were the ones invited into the sacred scene in the manger that night. And they were so impressed that they shared the news about it with others and gave glory to God for all that had happened.

One of my favorite Scriptures is verse 19: "But Mary treasured up all these things and pondered them in her heart." It had been quite a long day for her, possibly a long week or so, preparing for and then embarking on their trip. Add to that the stress of needing to find a place to stay to have the Baby, then realizing that an animal feeding trough was the best option. Right away they receive their first visitors, a strange group of excited shepherds. Amid it all we find her with that same humble attitude we saw on display when she heard she would bear Jesus. Instead of reacting negatively, she pondered all that happened and treasured the experience. Not all women would have been able to take all of that in stride. Mary was special. Somehow, she understood that the shepherds were a part of the bigger plan.

Luke 2:1-14: The Birth of Jesus

When we, like Mary, make the choice to trust God we should be ready for unique experiences. The arrival of the shepherds wasn't announced to her or Joseph, but still they came in all their angel-fueled excitement to be a part of all that was going on. God can use the simplest people and situations and make them divine just as He did at the manger that night. And we can see from the shepherds' story that God was faithful to His promise and that remains the same today.

Take some time to pray over all that you have just read.

_____

_____

_____

_____

_____

_____

_____

_____

_____

_____

_____

_____

The Christmas Story

Is there a verse that stands out to you as special in this passage?

_____
_____
_____
_____
_____
_____
_____

What is it about this verse that caught your attention?

_____
_____
_____
_____
_____
_____
_____
_____
_____
_____

Luke 2:1-14: The Birth of Jesus

Whether it's your first time to think about it or your hundredth time, what insights have you gleaned from the shepherds' story?

Journal your thoughts here.

_____

_____

_____

_____

_____

_____

_____

_____

_____

_____

_____

_____

_____

_____

_____

_____

From Matthew 2

After Jesus was born in Bethlehem in Judea, during the time of King Herod, Magi from the east came to Jerusalem ² and asked, "Where is the One who has been born king of the Jews? We saw His star when it rose and have come to worship Him."

³ When King Herod heard this he was disturbed, and all Jerusalem with him. ⁴ When he had called together all the people's chief priests and teachers of the law, he asked them where the Messiah was to be born. ⁵ "In Bethlehem in Judea," they replied, "for this is what the prophet has written:

⁶ "'But you, Bethlehem, in the land of Judah,
    are by no means least among the rulers of Judah;
    for out of you will come a ruler
    who will shepherd my people Israel.'[b]"

⁷ Then Herod called the Magi secretly and found out from them the exact time the star had appeared. ⁸ He sent them to Bethlehem and said, "Go and search carefully for the child. As soon as you find Him, report to me, so that I too may go and worship Him."

⁹ After they had heard the king, they went on their way, and the star they had seen when it rose went ahead of them until it stopped over the place where the Child was. ¹⁰ When they saw the star, they were overjoyed. ¹¹ On coming to the house, they saw the Child with His mother Mary, and they bowed down and worshiped Him. Then they opened their treasures and presented Him with gifts of gold, frankincense and myrrh. ¹² And having been warned in a dream not to go back to Herod, they returned to their country by another route.

The Christmas Story

No Christmas story could be complete without the Magi or Wisemen. Not much is known historically about them. Scholars have debated their precise country of origin and some traditions have given them names based on royalty in Eastern countries of the time. However, the Scripture gives us little detail. We don't even know for sure how many were. Most depictions of them shows three men dressed as royalty travelling on camels through the desert. We assume that the number of men comes from the three gifts that were presented, but men of such affluence and wealth would not have travelled so far in such a small group. They would have had an entourage. Their exact identity has little impact on their importance within the Christmas story. They were recognized as wise, had a passion for science and theological events, and the means to pursue their intellectual curiosity.

A lot happens in this section, including their visit with King Herod. Received by the king, the visitors were received when they asked about the location of the King of the Jews. What a surprise this must have been to Herod! He sought answers from his advisors who told him of the prophecy. He gave the Magi his secret message and they continued on their way. The wisemen travelled a great distance with good intentions, but Herod's interest in finding the Child is with evil purpose. Still, he didn't travel the short distance to find the Child. These foreigners had more passion and commitment to the task than he did.

Led once again by the star, the wisemen met Mary and Jesus. They presented Him with gifts, bowed down and worshipped Him. The gold, frankincense, and myrrh were gifts that would be presented to a king, thus signifying Jesus' status as King of the Jews. This was a foreshadowing of Jesus' ministry later. He began as an adult by teaching His people, as the shepherds did. This angered many as the news angered King Herod. Then later, His message was taken to foreigners who receive it gladly, as the Magi do.

From Matthew 2

It is human nature to lose sight of what we are after unless we stay focused. The trek of the wisemen is a great illustration about staying focused and motivated. It shows them following their passion. Their appetite for adventure took them from their homes and comforts, following only a star. Their curiosity propelled them over an unknown distance to welcome a Boy to the throne of a foreign people. That is an extreme amount of dedication. To make such a tremendous endeavor, they had to understand the significance of the One they were seeking.

This Boy was a king like no other. Not born in a palace and raised with servants nor destined to sit on an earthly throne. His destiny was far superior to anyone who has ever come before and will ever live after Him. His mission wasn't to overthrow kingdoms, but to save people from their sin and sinning, to make a way so that we can be pure. For those who seek Him, He is still the way.

Take some time to pray and contemplate the journey of the wisemen.

The Christmas Story

From Matthew 2

Have you ever felt that you could travel hundreds of miles because you were passionate about it?

Have you felt that way about Jesus?

_____

_____

_____

_____

_____

_____

_____

When was the last time you felt overjoyed with your relationship with Him?

_____

_____

_____

_____

_____

_____

_____

_____

From Matthew 2

If it has been a while or if you have never had a relationship with Him, ask God to kindle your fervor or restore the passion you once had. If you've never had it, ask Him to purify you and fill you with desires that are good and pleasing to Him. My prayer for you, dear reader, is that whatever your situation is, don't let your Christmas become about the wrong things, but like the wisemen, stay focused on the right things. And like the wisemen, that means finding Jesus, kneeling before Him, and worshipping Him alone.

Journal your thought here.

_____

_____

_____

_____

_____

_____

_____

_____

_____

_____

_____

_____

The Christmas Story